The Red Hijab

In this, her second book, Bonnie Bolling leaves no doubt as to her important place in America's contemporary poetry. You may read the deft aesthetic grace, as I did, as without misstep she navigates the strangeness of the land she inhabits. The inner heart that is revealed is true in its reflections; the world of the muezzin and hijab is seen through eyes that leave any judgment completely to the reader. All of her people resonate with remarkable depth and presence. There is no polemic here, no agenda, no travel narrative. *The Red Hijab* transcends all these. It is another remarkable book by Bolling, and it is a gift to us from a true artist.

    —Frank X. Gaspar

Like an ancient mantra, the steady patient voice in these poems threads through time and space and reworks the pattern of loss, such small and large violence, and a grief so communal and private its silence has sound. Always this sense of eternal *aftermath*. Yet there is cardamom for coffee, lemon in the gin, melons and good bread, the beautiful housemaid though "long ago, someone thought/ to carve away her ear." Yes, a stranger in a strange land here, but Bolling, an American poet in the Middle East, becomes a stranger to herself in the process—out of love and honest, fearless attention.

    —Marianne Boruch

The Red Hijab

Bonnie Bolling

winner of the John Ciardi Prize for Poetry
selected by H. L. Hix

BkMk Press
University of Missouri-Kansas City

BkMk Press
University of Missouri-Kansas City
5101 Rockhill Road
Kansas City, Missouri 64110
(816) 235-2558
www.umkc.edu/bkmk

Executive Editor: Robert Stewart
Managing Editor: Ben Furnish
Associate Editor: Michelle Boisseau
Assistant Managing Editor: Cynthia Beard

Cover photo: Shirin Neshat
        Rapture Series, 1999
        42 1/2 x 67 1/2 inches
        Photo taken by Larry Barns
        Copyright Shirin Neshat
        Courtesy Gladstone Gallery, New York and Brussels

Author photo: Rochelle Cocco

The John Ciardi Prize for Poetry wishes to thank Susan Cobin, Greg Field,
Lindsey Martin-Bowen, Linda Rodriguez, and Maryfrances Wagner.

BkMk Press wishes to thank Luke McKiddy and Cameron Morse.

ISBN 978-1-943491-06-3

Library of Congress Cataloging-in-Publication Data

Names: Bolling, Bonnie, author.
Title: The red hijab / Bonnie Bolling.
Description: Kansas City, Missouri : BkMk Press, 2016.
Identifiers: LCCN 2016045578 | ISBN 9781943491063 (alk. paper)
Classification: LCC PS3602.O566 A6 2016 | DDC 811/.6--dc23 LC record
available at https://lccn.loc.gov/2016045578

Contents

Foreword by H. L. Hix   7

I

The Red Hijab   13
In Diraz   14
56 Degrees Centigrade   16
The Compound   17
Grace, a Moment of   18
Broken   20
One Good Man   22
Maybe, That Good Cherry Jam   24
The Going   25
Above the *Azan*   27
Together, We Stagger   29
Lost   30
Gathering Plumeria   32

II

Nourishment   35
Stars, Moon, Rooster   37
Shamaal   38
Noon   40
Ninety-Nine Beautiful Names   43
All Day, a Certain Terrible Beauty   45
Blood, Money   47
A Silencing   49
Only Bread, Only Water   51
My Blood Is Already on Your Feet,   54
They Say There's No Arabic Word for Love   55
The Missing Alleluia   57

III

Sometimes, You Shut out the Fire   61
Close Call   62
Happiness, Almost   64
And Then, Night Again,   65
On a Balcony with the *Lunch Poems*   68

Acknowledgments

Much gratitude and appreciation to the journals where many of these poems first appeared.

But Who's Counting, A "Poetry Matters" Anthology (Los Nietos Press)
"The Missing Alleluia"
Consequence Magazine "Only Bread, Only Water"
The Lampeter Review "The Going," "Above the *Azan*,"
"On a Balcony With the *Lunch Poems*"
Miramar "Somethimes You Shut out the Fire," "Nourishment," "Grace, A
Moment Of," "Blood, Money"
New Letters "Close Call," "In Diraz," "Ninety-Nine Beautiful Names,"
"Shamaal"
The Persian Book Review "56 Degrees Centigrade"
Solo Novo "One Good Man," "Together, We Stagger,"
"All Day, a Certain Terrible Beauty"
The Southern Review "The Red Hijab," "The Compound," "Broken,"
"Maybe, That Good Cherry Jam," "Lost," "Gathering Plumeria,"
"Stars, Moon, Rooster"
Verdad "Noon"

The author is thankful and grateful for the Bread Loaf Bakeless Camargo Residency Fellowship, for the time and the place to write poems.

The author celebrates the many poets, and others, with whom this book is in conversation.

Foreword

The pressure on media venues to secure and retain a large audience ensures that the news made available through them is heavily biased toward attention-getting conflict and violence, with the result that if, say, a member of one race or religion kills a member of another race or religion, the event will be widely reported, but if two members of different races or religions work together to start a community garden in their neighborhood, the event likely will go unnoticed and untold.

Poetry can contest that bias, and Bonnie Bolling's *The Red Hijab* does. Late in the book, the poem "On a Balcony with the *Lunch Poems*" makes that counterambition explicit. "This in the news today:" the poem offers, followed by two examples of dramatic conflict. But that brief news synopsis is followed immediately by a "Meanwhile . . ." The events reported in the news were true, and the conflicts they manifested were real, but so were the events that only the poem reported:

> Meanwhile . . . a woman lifts
>   her *niqab* and sips. Smoldering
> tires. Someone's unloading yams.
>
> I get up to find the toilet.
>   The *azan* pierces the afternoon,
> a lost nuthatch panics on the railing.

Of what happens in the Middle East, most North Americans receive little word except for what news media present. Consequently, the most readily available image of the Middle East is biased toward conflict and violence. Bonnie Bolling, because she lives part of each year in Diraz, a village in Bahrain, is in position to offer, and does offer in *The Red Hijab*, alternative dispatches. Bolling does not pose in these poems as an "unacknowledged legislator" with a solution to global political problems. *The Red Hijab* does not pretend divine perspective, and does not purport to have an answer to the conflicts reported in the news. It does, though, adopt an alternative form of attention and offer an alternative kind of account.

One result of that alternative approach is that these poems present a more complex portrait than the news presents. It is still the case that in them sometimes "Someone's throwing bottles / filled with gasoline," but in Bolling's poems, unlike the news, "there's also a chicken / cooking in the kitchen." In these poems there are still "sounds / of shooting down in the village," but there is also a young boy, suffering in suffocating mid-day heat during Ramadan, but spitting because "Only the most righteous / do not swallow their own water."

The Red Hijab will not bring about world peace, but it offers one of poetry's most generous gifts: it sees more, and more clearly, than the nightly news sees, and it offers that richer, clearer sight to its readers.

H. L. Hix

for John, my sons, and for the villagers

—for I have been a stranger in a strange land.
—Exodus 2:22

I

*Red was the sun's most beautiful throne and all the
other colors prayed on red rugs.*
                                   —Adonis

The Red Hijab

Persian Gulf

A hard rain falling on the corrugated roof
of the abandoned double-wide
across the steaming street,
its tangle of razor wire and oleander,
the rotting porch, cats prowling underneath
and mewing from branches
of the long-dead acacia tree
and I've been at my desk
all morning, upstairs in the loft,
the windows streaked and pocked
with drops and rivulets
and the ring-necked doves
all lined up under the eaves,
wings folded and feathers fluffed.
This place is as old as anything.
Every kind of person has traveled through.
Every animal and bird and weapon
so these days, only rain is remarkable.
I am watching the trash-picking man,
his head wrapped in a potato sack
his shoulders buttressing the clouds,
dragging his bin down the cobbles,
driveway to driveway, rain
beading down to the tip of his nose
and then a housemaid passing by,
basket of laundry in one hand
opened umbrella in the other,
her brown face turned down
but her red hijab a damp smudge
of brightness moving, in relief,
against the bruising sky.

In Diraz

The first heat of the year pressing in, heavy
like a hurricane, coming down hard
and then the *azan*, pushing again, creeping in
doing its work so I've come to expect it,
to wait for it; this is a place where if you want
a chair you have to pay a man to make one.
Sometimes the birds talk to me, also the nameless cat
claiming his small dry patch under the hedgerow —
he among us who bears no shame also has no love
and outside these village walls — the world, oh, the world
and inside them are no bullet trains, no sounds of alleluia
only the sun devouring every corner, only a man
rolling up the creaking metal storefront
another who is washing his feet, then he is kneeling,
praying before taking his lunch and a woman
is sweeping the ancient's dust into a bin
staring hard at her work, breathing her story into the stony air
and here I stand on the corner, leaning next to the sign
that says in three languages: *no uncovered women allowed*
adjusting and re-adjusting my black hijab, me —
on this narrow, broken footpath keeping my silence and my distance
because whoever my gods are, they're surely wrong for this place, me —
across from the bright gold and blue tiled mosque — Shi'ite
not Sunni. Sunni mosques are made of pale stone.
No one's looking at me but everyone's looking away from me,
even the woman, oh — there is no fooling her.
The market had no meat today, only the hind quarters
of a sheep swinging on a hook so another salad
will do tonight with some lentils and bread.
Tomatoes are good here — despite everything
they pay attention to vegetables. My home is not here

but I don't think it's there either, and my children
are not here. They are *there*, eating pancakes in the kitchen
or listening to music or maybe they are kissing someone
but *here* in Diraz, in front of this old doorway
a villager stands up from his praying,
folds away his small carpet and starts making a broom.

56 Degrees Centigrade

The sun keeps.
A boy near the broken arch of a juice stall,
beating a stick against the crumbling wall.
Everywhere, a Friday afternoon
in August, but here in the village
also the final week of Ramadan.
Hour after hour after dry, fomented hour,
shahada crying from the minaret.
No reading allowed, except the Qu'ran.
So long the boy's been waiting,
wanting to fast. He's old enough now.
Black flags whip in the wind.
The boy gazes at a pitcher of juice,
salivates, spits it out.
He turns back to beating his stick,
stops, squares his shoulders,
looks around, then starts again.
He is pleased with himself.
Only the most righteous
do not swallow their own water.

The Compound

Smoke's blowing down from the village again,
but here in the yard, plumeria blooms drop,
unfolding carpets for the skeletal cat
who nearly dies daily, and for the American
who sips wine or lavender tea,
who wears Spanx tight against her alabaster skin.
In the village, a mother kneels
in the dust and wrings a chicken's neck.
She wants to be heard, is all.
Last night, before they took him away
her son stood here. He was a listener.
Maybe they've untied the ropes
by now and tended to his broken bones.
But who will remember this boy,
his mother's grieving or her chickens
scrabbling inside these beaten walls?
The muezzin makes the air swollen.
Palm fronds cast knife-edged shadows
over the American, who is backstroking
across the long, blue water.

Grace, a Moment of

I sleep until the eastern sky
is on fire, until the sound
of the muezzin's voice.
The room unfolds
when I open my eyes.
I want to pray, I think,
I am going to pray,
I am going to try again.
I assume the position:
knees bent, face pressed
and I wait. They said to wait.
Wait for what, I asked.
Something, they said, *you will know.*
The sun-slants deepen
and cover me. I hold very still.
But the images pass through again—
the old Indian with a cloth on his head,
tying rope around his creaking cart
of useless rubble, the fuming
sheik in the vegetable souk
with his wives, and that woman—
the one who fell in love,
buried to her neck,
face down in the dirt
after the first stone.
Who among us will bear witness?
Oh, the regret.
Poor American.
How guilty you are.
How the world despises you.

Something, it seems,
must be given now,
something precious—
maybe that lamb stumbling
in the back of the speeding
pickup truck in Diraz.
My children are not a part of this;
they are not to blame.
Pure silk, this small carpet is,
knotted by a family in Iran.
Save them, I say from the floor, *save them all.*

Broken

The wound is the place where the Light enters you.
—Rumi

I go to the market,
though many are missing
from their homes in the village.

I take the small car
and do not think about children
with no food or mothers
who want to feed them.
The apples are good today.

I buy a kilo of the red kind,
grown twelve thousand kilometers from here,
and place them in my basket.

I go out for lunch and listen
to one of the Americans complain
how her neighbor
has a bigger and better something.
We discuss the heat
and the film
playing at the cinema.
I don't mention
the tear gas late into the night
or my despair over
a son, back home, who has lost
his way again.

Isn't it important to stay empty,
to remain unfulfilled,
to be a kind of *negative force*,
or *to become something broken*
that cannot break further?
Otherwise, how will I take part
in the life of this swallowtail
butterfly, born with three wings?

One Good Man

Again I'm awakened by doves
murmuring at the window
and the sound of the boy
with the broken face
sweeping his palm frond;
the morning light's pouring,
persimmon trees and petunias—
but this is not a place for perfection:
earlier tanks rolling into Manama
and now every villager praying and washing
washing, praying. The school's on fire.
Children are kicking balls
against rolled-down store fronts
in the terrible streets,
mothers are wailing and cooking
cooking, wailing and everyone's waiting
for news. The markets, the ATM—all stopped,
the death toll rising yet the king
declaring *all is well*,
the newspaper proclaiming
only rapture, tirelessly seeking
some false translation
that might suddenly lift
this despair to a place of beauty.
But what about those of us here
too numb or broken, and *without*
a written plea? The *azan* entering us
again, again, insisting we still must face
the greatest jihad: that struggle
against ourselves. Muhammad
once told of an angel

who was sent by God
to destroy a city but the angel,
refusing to do so, was asked why.
I found one good man, the angel said,
who prays and fasts and praises God,
although he keeps to himself
and does nothing more.
Well then, God replied
to the upturned faces,
destroy him first. Outside,
a low hedge grows
in faultless obedience,
desiring nothing
and the housemaid last night,
face down with her praying
and today I wake
and break fast with cries
of nesting doves,
and then the muezzin calling
from the nearest minaret,
all the voices echoing,
tumbling into one another again—
but nothing answering.

Maybe, That Good Cherry Jam

If a single day in the life
of an ordinary woman
is enough, if it includes
at the beginning strong
coffee with cardamom,
or maybe a squeeze of lemon
in a cup of gin—depends on the day,
no one has said yet what kind
of day this actually is,
it might be the most ordinary
day of anyone's life: that light
through the kitchen window,
the ironed cloth, warm bread
and some good, cherry jam
or a sip of gin held tight
for a moment against
the back of the tongue,
her heart already used up
by some wreckage or other;
they say the world breaks everyone,
that what you become
afterward is all that really matters
so, then why shouldn't she put down
this day, like a bundle,
and just walk away?

The Going

We wake too late and find the roundabout
already crowded: protesters, tear gas
and the Pakistani unloading melons.
Rubber bullets thunk past—
they've formed a human chain
all the way to Budaiya,
and soon we'll have to go.
The kitchen is too warm
where we are drinking coffee
thick with grated cardamom,
and outside the window there's shouting,
occasional waves of birdsong.
The housemaid, who will stay behind,
is ironing. She glances up,
not anxious but shaking
her big, beautiful head,
says *big noisey* and adjusts her hijab.
Long ago, someone thought
to carve away her left ear.

On one side of this island
is a long peninsula and I have walked it.
The Persian Gulf on one side,
the Arabian Sea on the other.
Every kind of flower is here.
Every bird. There's a humming,
a watery music coming
from the stand of beach palms,
with its rustling fronds
and nosegay of dates.
Oh, there are times when

you want to lay everything down
just to see all of it at once,
raw and shining, brilliant in the sand
but it's better if you don't.
Yesterday, when the house water
was brown, I cut some lilies
and put them in a vase.
Today the water is still brown
but make no mistake, the going
is never easy. Sometimes it's hard
not to fall in love with false joys
but you can take yourself
out of yourself—
you can close your eyes
for a moment and not breathe,
and then you can gaze in at yourself.
Will you see beauty?
Maybe you'll see nothing.
When it is time, I hug the housemaid.
Take what you need, I say into her good ear,
do what you have to. But she is only smiling.

Above the *Azan*

Some days start already torn to shreds,

    stripped and cold, like rain falling

confusedly outside some broken-down doorway.

    Old flowers grow wild around the birdbath.

Weeds. Sand. What makes people behave

    as though they were the ones who fought

the actual war? The bougainvillea canes

    have bent fully over, but are still shining,

blown red and trembling with bees.

    I begin lifting them. Above the *azan*,

I hear a woman weeping.

    Even in this part of the world

a woman's life is fraught.

    Even here, there comes a time

when the only thing left to do

    is to remake yourself, resurrect.

A long thorn pierces my finger and it bleeds,

      but I cut the best branches and bring them

into the cooled, marbled villa.

      I water them, give them a glass vase,

a place on the polished front hall table.

      The housemaid lifts her eyes from her work

and gives me that look:

      Oh, we want it all, don't we?

Together, We Stagger

Late sun, broken bottles
embedding the high wall,
black flags flying from kiosks—
black means Shi'ite, also grief
and smoke ribbons out like silk.
The men are burning the village again.
They are trying to tell the world
something but no one is listening.
Maybe they are saying that we all stagger
from some false, collective wound or another.
Oh, it's been this way too long, they're saying.
Only together will the healing start.
Some of them will die tonight.
This has been accepted. Already
police have lined up. Already
tear gas has been issued, forcing
them back into the rooms
of their untranslatable lives.
All day, a boy, his pockets
filled with stones. All day,
a woman stays home
because even a rusted tub
that needs scrubbing is reason enough.
Anything to keep away the waiting
and anyway, how little it is you truly need to live.
We could trade places, she
and I, but when that final tempest
heaves, which one of us will be spared?
The Pakistani wearing a bright cloth
waits. Soon the men go to him, and he opens a melon.
Together they eat, watching the flames,
the terrible smoke, and in the distance
is the faint crow of a rooster.

Lost

in the spice souk

I am holding a tiny dried lemon
and breathing the scent
of a hundred vanilla beans.
Crows pant on the overhead wire.
Men wait and lean in the sun,
some smoking, some just sitting
and the covered woman
next to me adjusts her hijab.
A hot wind gusts through—
as though to raise the dead,
pulling it loose from her head.
Everything, it seems,
has led up to this moment.
This is one of those times
just before the waiting stops,
when we're made to cross over
into what we've been waiting for.
This very place, it is told and told,
was the heart of paradise
until judgment came down
but you know how that story goes.
Aren't we all made to tremble
together, and cling to the edge
of the same soaring, burning battlement?
You can't stop this from happening
no matter what false part of yourself
you've been surrendering, despite glass
after glass of chardonnay. Even the village boy
casting his stones knows this—
you can read the old stories in his eyes

if you are lucky and he lifts them to you.
In the gutter a pile of bleached rubble shifts.
The uncovered woman stands there alone,
shoulders braced against what comes next
and I gaze into the bright cathedral
of her face, but she is only staring down.

Gathering Plumeria

I waited until the heat was nearly down
to cut the nosegay of dates from the palm.
I was starting on the plumeria boughs
when it happened. It was the stray cat, is all,
going along the high wall with a kitten
in her mouth that set it off, that thing
about what living in this place might
be doing to me. I heated up yesterday's
soup and brought it to the rooftop,
watching the villagers opening their lights.
After, I found myself out in the mottled
darkness gathering the fallen blossoms
into my arms. It was very late.
There was the smell of tear gas
again and I could hear sounds
of shooting down in the village.
When you somehow are being chosen
for something larger than yourself
but do not feel equal to it,
you must become the person who
can do it. That is, I believe, how it
works. In this part of the world, I am
not hurrying, but I'm growing strange
under these backward stars. I am watching
the cat nursing her son, watching the old women
in the old village watching me. I am taking
it all in, every side because stories
from the heart don't lie.
These blossoms are not a burden.
They are always pure in their brief time
with us, and so, have no regrets when they are finished.
They are the color of the moon.

II

Where were you when I laid the foundation of the earth?
. . . when the morning stars sang together and all the
sons of God shouted for joy?
                                        —Job 38:4-7

I read the book of Job last night—I don't think God comes
out well in it.
                                        —Virginia Woolf

Nourishment

The American has gone out
to look for oil and gas.
His wife waits, at the small desk
near the window.
The keyboard makes its tapping
sounds as she moves her fingers.
Outside: the sun.
Nearby, blond houses
with backyard pools
and the other Americans.
They hardly exist for her.
This is dangerous, she knows,
to feel this way because soon
the time will come when
she'll need them.
She's always been this way.
There's a particular nourishment
in her solitude. The rooster
sounds off from across the stony road.
Through the eyepiece
she sees the yellow field—
black prayer flags whipping
and smoke blowing down
from the village again.
She considers van Gogh
and all those sunflowers.
A slight twist of the lens
brings it all together:
the crowded white stones,

dried reeds and grasses,
the flames, and the nosegay
of young girls spilling from school,
their bright headscarves catching the wind
and their brown faces, terrified,
lifted to the heaving light.

Stars, Moon, Rooster

Later, the road looked bright
from the kitchen window,
so she walked it.
Stars, moon. The sand.
The rooster still awake.
Then the village —
some small houses
with dark squares of glass,
the kind of house with linoleum,
with a woman who stays up late and hopes.
She knows about hope, has had plenty.
But the hoping for a thing is always
so much more than the thing itself.
A child is born and becomes
the embodiment of hope.
She'd seen *that* kind before.
But what then?
A moment or two of purity,
naked on a table,
then the whole thing thrust
into the arms of another?
In the end, it all gets used up.
And the hope doesn't matter so much
anymore, and anyway, she's come far
enough by now, been gone long enough.
A mix of sea salt and wind scuttles up dust,
an empty plastic grocery sack.
She goes to that blown-down cyclone fence,
steps over and crosses into the desert.
She heads to the open place
where light falls equally, like snow,
where everything's a shivering
kismet of silvery white.

Shamaal

And then winds again,
coming from the north,
bringing a crust of pink,
like snow, like ice
so you have to take a shovel to it.
After that, the rains.
Who said every common thing
that comes to us is a blessing,
gone unnoticed, until taken away?
We live the lives we live
not the ones we dream
and soon enough
we'll lie beneath it all
so better to insist
while there's still time.
Like the young boys wearing black,
gathering beneath the village arch.
They're restless again.
You can tell by their eyes
they'll stop at nothing this time.
Though slim-hipped
and bony-shouldered,
together they could overturn
my small car, but instead
they go after the old Pakistani.
They cast their stones.
And then, because a mother's love
isn't enough, they take him
down in the burning street.
All of this makes a great
and terrible debacle but,

even so, the boys look away.
Bored of this game, they trace
bare toes through wet dust.
They wait between supper and the flames,
ignoring the bright tongues at work.
They hug themselves. They stare at the rain.

Noon (Al Dhuhr)

for Wisława Szymborska

*Lo! God has bought from the believers their lives and their
wealth because the Garden will be theirs . . .*
                    —Qur'an 9:111

He'll put on the vest at noon.
But first, he'll walk his sister to school
and buy bread for the house at the market.
She waits on a stool in the kitchen.
She's young—no breasts to speak of yet.
She salts her egg, drinks a cup of milk.

It's only nine fifteen. Still plenty of time.
They walk side by side in the cool breath of morning,
a used book in her hand, ballet slippers—
and the unused vest in his.
The vest's not heavy, maybe the weight
of a couple of stones or a soccer ball.
The school's not far—it faces the sea,
a school for girls, with religious women who teach.
His sister kisses his cheek, turns away, goes inside.
Her eyes are blue.

Now, it is ten twenty three.
He stands in line under an incandescent
lamp at the bakery. He tears a warm chunk
from the loaf and inhales the aroma,
breathing it in again, again, his senses
swelling with butter and yeast,
but he does not eat it. They said not to eat.
His father had loved bread with honey.

(His mother has died.)
His sister has blue eyes.

The time is now eleven twenty five.
Men have gathered in the street.
Some are talking. Some are laughing.
And there are those teenagers, wearing t-shirts
and jeans, clapping to a radio, sitting at tables.
They go in and out of the café for small paper cups of tea.
A one-armed man with a full, white beard nods, smiles, goes inside.

It is eleven forty seven. He is not afraid of the vest.
He has a higher purpose. He is fortunate to be chosen.
The reward is great and soon will be his.
He deserves this. (There is nothing else.)

Eleven fifty and twenty five seconds.
He looks at the vest. It is made of good cloth,
canvas and wool. An important zipper is
sewn down the front and generous pockets
are stitched inside, filled with plastic
explosives and wire.
There is also a round, flat button.

Eleven fifty eight. Almost time.
He lets go of the bread and puts on the vest,
zips it up, puts his hands in the pockets.
The vest feels comfortable, soft like old skin.
It smells of sewing machine oil. Gingerly,
he fingers the smooth face of the button.

No, not yet. Still too soon.
In the ancient village, the café bustles.
Long black flags on rooftops snap in the breeze.
And that one-armed man from before,
the one with the beard, pedals away
on a rusted bicycle. Good for him.

The time is eleven fifty nine and twenty two seconds.
There is a group of them leaning and smoking.
He tells the fat, bald one about his sister,
whose eyes are blue as heaven.
So are yours, the fat, bald one replies, blowing
smoke from his mouth in rings. *So are yours*.

Finally, it is noon. He is not unhappy or unloved.
He does not live in squalor, or out on the streets
but these days, it seems not even a king has any hope to spare.
A pity that bus pulls over, stopping at the curb,
letting those people get off—

Ninety-Nine Beautiful Names

He will be like rain falling on a mown field, like
showers watering the earth.
—Psalm: 72:6

It was one of those nights

when I would drink a cup of coffee—

black, with a splash of something strong and brown,

upstairs, in my own small darkness,

where I'd consider the many names of Allah.

There are no likenesses for Allah,

for how to carve something

that embodies all things,

yet in the most abstract way?

There isn't a name

that says One Who

Is Strong Like The Oak.

There is only One Who

Is Most Jealous, or One Who

Withholds.

Today, in her kitchen,

a woman set herself on fire.

With gasoline.

They say it was done

in the name of Allah,

the Absolute and All-Knowing.

Others say she only

wanted to drive the car.

I press my hand

against the blue square

of window, gazing out

at gleaming limbs of the olive tree.

It is raining again

and the moon's light

impales each raindrop, falls,

and every leaf

and flower is golden.

All Day, a Certain, Terrible Beauty

All day they were burning
American flags in the village
and smoke blew over the sea
with a certain, terrible beauty.
Meanwhile, at the market
sheep swung on hooks,
their shorn skulls about the size
of my son's foot,
and lentils were in burlap sacks.
I bought a half-kilo of the red ones
and drove home the back way,
past the King's camels.
My friend, Isa, says one country's
already been destroyed.
And now another one?
He was looking at me.
I did not know what to say.
His eyes spoke without words
that he knows what I don't.
Had he said it with words
I wouldn't believe him.
His wife, Maryam, excuses herself for prayer.
I think, no, I have not always lived right
though I've tried. I've done what's expected
and more, but there's never enough.
No one can help each and all,
though there's always the trying to
and so, a thing was done
because I could not help it.
How small a thing can seem at first,

how long it can keep on.
I park the car. The kitchen door
is unlocked—
they will burn your flag
but they won't steal.
It could cost them a hand.
In the large country 20 kilometers west,
they sever hands and heads, and put out eyes,
they cast their stones on Thursday
so they can enjoy Holy Day.
Tomorrow is Christmas Eve.

Blood, Money

If an angel comes to this window
where I gaze out at the sun,
where I watch the white horse
running, I will not be afraid
but I will not let him in.
For if you do, nothing's the same.
Fear not, is what angels usually say,
but that doesn't matter much.
Even if you believe him
every single thing keeps.
Don't blame him—
he's only doing his job.
We are safe here, I say out loud,
in case he is out there,
and it's true. We have what we need.
I am eating flat bread.
A man bakes it in a stone hole,
sells it in an alley. Yesterday
I drove the small car there and got out.
Cats roamed the sand lot.
I rounded the narrow alleys
until I found the men's tea stall.
I can't have tea there,
but I can buy my bread,
walk around and eat it.
The bread-maker, who wore a red skullcap
and something resembling a plaid tablecloth
gave bread to me hot
in a waxed sheet of paper.
I bit into it. This kind of bread
does not even need butter.
I gave him some silver coins
with magic lamps on them.
He is from some other place,

just about everyone here who does work is.
But those skeletal cats are born here,
and the white horse too, resting his long face now,
on a low limb of the acacia,
just as the sun, a bloody cloth
in the anemic sky, is making its way
over to wake *my* children,
who were born in the village of *me*.
But the young flag-burners
are born here, in *these* villages.
Their hair is thick and black.
They have luminous eyes.
They smoke in the dark
at a young age and make their own weapons.
(Sometimes, they name their bombs:
Ritz-Carlton, Fifth Fleet,
American Avenue.)
A favorite manner of killing
is to inject air into someone's veins.
Untraceable, is what they say.
They say that boys
carry small carpets
from their rooms
and lay them down
on worn stones inside
a blown-out mosque.
There's also liquor.
And the village girls
join them, and uncover.
Oh, everywhere, so much yearning.
And what is the cost of this yearning?
Well, a gallon of gas is a dollar.

A Silencing

A fish bleeds in the pan,
the gas stove is hissing,
there's news on the plastic radio.
I sing a little and put onion
into hot oil, mince
a green chili, wash rice.
Deep in the village
the blind rooster's
crowing. This village
is said to be ancient.
Been the same for centuries,
they say, except for air conditioning.
I think about people starting here
and later ending, year after year
speaking in that old way of the desert,
praying together in the terrible heat.
Not the younger ones though.
They are saying other things.
They are staying out late now,
despite the curfew.
They have taken to hiding in the shadows.
Someone, the news is claiming,
is telling them to do it.
Someone from outside is fooling them
into going up against each other.
I slice a tomato.
I think about that line in a poem,
It is a small country.
There is nothing one man
will not do to another.
The muezzin had just finished Isha'a,

the news is saying.
He was walking home in the dark,
fingering the worn tissue paper of his Qu'ran.
But he didn't need to refer to it much,
now that he'd memorized it.
It had taken half his life to do that.
I cook the fish and set it on the oval platter.
Then the rice, steaming in little bowls. Arugula.
Everyone sitting at the table now
and someone says grace.
His mother, says the news,
had asked him to bring a goat
for *qurbani* (sacrifice)
to give *sadqa* (charity),
to keep away the evil eye.
But she spoke too late.
He never saw them coming.
Then, they were on him.
Do it, someone said, *do it now*.
So, they did it with scissors.
They cut-out his tongue—

Only Bread, Only Water

*Well, then, eliminate the people, curtail them,
force them to be silent.*
    —Dostoevsky

We spend another morning

   in the outdoor market

looking for the man

   who bakes bread in a stone hole.

We nod and he nods,

   but so many stories separate us.

So many nations.

   We search with our tongues,

desperate for a phrase, some scrap

   of language or utterance

that will allow our worlds

   to come together for a moment,

but there are no words, except bread.

   And maybe water. Last night

the man sleeping in the yard,

the garden hose dripping

near his mouth; he knows

a kind of bread. We wake him,

and for what? Are you okay,

we ask. Can we help you?

He says nothing but his face

tells the same, terrible story.

Yesterday, a friend from the states

wrote to ask if we're safe.

I also didn't know how to answer.

Are any of us safe, I am thinking,

all of us in places gone the way

of some infected consciousness.

Is it possible things might be too far gone?

We bring our bread to a small,

stone *majlis*. We go in, sit down.

It is cool inside. We've brought a box

of small candles. We eat the bread,

sip water from plastic bottles.

Last week, in this small country,

they dragged a man through the alley.

He knew bread from yet another place.

They made a wooden cage for him.

And then, with many needles and

syringes filled with heroin,

they killed him.

We light one candle for him,

another for the world.

My Blood Is Already on Your Feet,

(after cutting myself
on the metal doorjamb . . .)

so why not share this blood-red
Pakistani carrot with me,
the one with the dirt still clinging?
And what about this tomato from Jordan —
it is small, but it's red and it's heirloom, after all.
Only these dates are local
but I've heard you can buy a box of lettuces
that grow in the holes of a wall in a blown-out mosque.
No soil is used, only air and water
because even soil must come here on a ship,
from some other place, through the Strait of Hormuz
which has been shut-down.
I mop the blood from the kitchen floor.
I unlock the bottle of gin.
I mention that famishing man from Kashmir,
the one who works on the stadium?
They've refused him his wages,
taken away his passport and visa.
Still, he washes and irons his shirt each evening
before he lies down on a mat, in a room
shared with a dozen other men.
Well, you say to me, chipping
away at a bag of ice, *at least he is not alone.*

They Say There's No Arabic Word for Love

There are ants who live with me.
I have to get down on the floor to watch them.
Right now, they are using their front pairs of arms
to carry a single crumb across the cracked tile.
There appears to be one who's in charge,
who seems to be quickstepping back and forth,
maybe inciting them. Even so they're quiet
and polite about the whole thing and after
they've gone back to their small kingdom
I climb the stairs to where I work,
hunched over books and these lines,
dismantling the heart. Yes, love
lives there but so does all its enemies.
These things are small also, yet batter
the heart's rooms like a blinding snow.
No word for love?
Maybe it's just too difficult to say.
Everyone knows this.
And everyone knows to pick beans
when the afternoon is dry.
Oh, the heart will give what it can
but you must be careful.
You must give something
back or it will fool you.
Like picking the rusted bean.
Sometimes you don't realize
until the whole bushel's gone bad.
And the heart, it might even win,
might break you further
if such a thing is possible,

and that's the worst.
But all the small things,
and ghosts of those things
come and go, and some are bound
to stay a while, like the ants.
What can you do
when all your rooms grow
terribly dark, when winter
turns its back on you,
when even your own breath feels cold?
You can spray the ants
or you can light a lamp
and lie down with them.
Maybe they'll hear the small rumble
in the shuttered cellar of your heart—
they'll listen as well as anyone.

The Missing Alleluia

America

You're coming home and it's raining,
coming home to church bells
and a choir that's singing.
The steeple is shining.

You're standing and waiting
under the coffee shop's green awning.
There's no bomb-maker here, wearing a vest.
No, someone is laughing, unbroken by the call to prayer.
Here the market sells pork chops and wine,
women aren't covering—they look a man straight in the eye.
Breasts are encouraging.

You see someone you're sure you know
so you're waving, smiling, but no one's remembering.
You're an outsider now,
holding her sandwich and beer,
alone in a bar with its sports and day-drinking
and the polished mahogany and oh,
those vast deserts of time
you've crossed over, to get home,
and always that war down below.

Yes, you think, *there is something missing here.*

Outside, a man opens his umbrella
and then he's running, bent over low,

shouldering what he's been given.
Yes, you have to go down deep to find it.
Underneath the light. Under the prayer.
Beyond words and wine and all the goddamn smiling

and then, it's there. The missing alleluia.
It comes to you quietly as you walk home,
breathing in scents of earthworms and geraniums,
watching the clouds in the distance—violet and scudding,
bleeding into the sea, and the rain sequined on the streets.

III

But listen to me. For one moment quit being sad.
Hear blessings dropping their blossoms around you.
—Rumi

Sometimes, You Shut out the Fire

Someone's throwing bottles
filled with gasoline,
plugged with silk torn
from his *umm*'s hijab.
Fire's everywhere. Tear gas.
Guards with shields and guns
six-deep in formation,
the sheer nothingness of the ground,
and those workers from India
are hanging themselves.
It feels like the day after
the day the towers went down.

But, we're told we are meant
to enjoy our lives,
so there's also a chicken
cooking in the kitchen,
and the sounds of Bocelli
singing beneath a full moon.
We can't make heaven
with our own hands—
there is only the trying to.
Sometimes, I stay home. But not today.
Sometimes, you have to shut out the fire.

Close Call

*—when, sick for home, she stood in
tears amid the alien corn.*
—Keats

Meanwhile, today the yard
feels empty so I go out
and buy a trellis
and a vine to put with it.
I dig the hole. I hit the nail.
The hammer makes a sharp
pinging that floods the desert
and then keeps true,
going out over the sea
like an ill wind at night
that makes you sit
straight up in bed.
I'm alone so much now
my own voice startles me,
like rain in the dark,
I greet the moon each night.
Sometimes I despise the stars—
always they're crowding
around my friend, the moon.
Always they look down on me.
I plant seeds beyond
their expiry date
just for possibility,
just so something's coming.

I think about that other life:
is it still going on without me
or has it somehow stopped,
and now there's only this one?
You sound nutty again,
is what someone from home
says, and I worry it's the truth.
Holding the nail in one hand
and the hammer in the other,
there's that same unraveling,
when you hear only your own heart's keening
until finally the rooster's crow
two stony roads over reaches me,
and I nod and breathe and come back.
The hammer meets the nail again.
I think of its brightness traveling
over this desperate landscape,
over the rooster and mothers
grieving for lost sons,
and then reaching the choirs,
the silence of before.

Happiness, Almost

Maghrib again. The lingering
white heat. I sit alone in the half-light,
waiting. I can almost taste it.
Almost. I'm worried
I've lost it for good,
and already I'm ashamed
about my next hangover,
but I have to smile
when I remember meeting
Mona Lisa that first time,
before she was bullet-proofed,
before she was glassed-in, touched-up.
I remember a carafe of something cheap
in the dining car and how
Picassos are best seen
on a long, Paris afternoon
when it's raining.
There you are—like when your milk lets down.

And Then, It's Night Again,

Sometimes my life opened its eyes in the dark.
—Tomas Tranströmer

and here *I* am again—wine in my cup,
my flannel gown, alone in the kitchen
searching for something
to crack open this same darkness
that keeps bullying me.
I stare at it through the window
and pretend not to notice,
that I don't mind it being here,
but of course it knows.
It wants to fool me.
I ignore this parlor trickery,
put my pen to the paper, and look away.
Suffer the darkness,
the Lord insists, and I do,
(*though it won't take away sins*).
Darkness can blind you to this world
and mine is waiting for me.
It wants to embrace me,
maybe it wants to devour me
but I won't go to it—
not now, not while I am sitting
at this linoleum counter
reading Rumi, sipping
a buttery Chardonnay,
hearing the house hum and click.
Have you met your darkness?
Well, mine is crafty
and I mean to ask it something.
This is a sharp-witted darkness

that much I can tell
but like an impatient lover,
will tolerate only a question or two.
And so I ask: what exactly *did* God
say to the rose to cause it to laugh
in full-blown beauty?
Oh, I know I have been lazy.
A gift of lilies fades on their stems,
the apples turn in their basket,
the house water is brown.
But even worse, books mingle
on the cracked, tiled floor —
poetry sprawling alongside fiction.
Plath lying down with Faulkner.
Surely this is a good thing
and I do think Faulkner would be pleased —
after all, who wouldn't be lured by a black so blue,
so cunning, you ache to go to it?
And why *not* hold the pale, dying hands
of all the Addie Bundrens in the world?
Who in *that* slanting house of sorrow
and sweat did not love her?
Darkness came for them
and make no mistake, it will come for you.
Like moonlight unleafing the desert,
it will hunt you down,
unearth you in your own room.
And that is when I hope to hear
a whisper in *my* heart.
Sometimes you can hear it
late at night if you listen for it
which is what I am doing now.

It's pure rapture, like how the rose felt.
That's what this darkness is saying tonight.
It's saying you can spin and spin
wearing skirts braided with golden thread
and all the bright colors of this world,
and you can even lie down in your clean,
lace gown, which you carefully
stitched during all the long hours,
but there is no sampling, no small taste.
It's either you're in or you're out.
Like when I wanted to cross over,
just for a moment. But the current there
is very strong. And once you are there
it cloaks you in velvet and silk
and then suddenly you are thrust away,
with or without shoes,
and of course you are smiling.
You won't want to ever leave it
so better not to go at all,
and anyway, there's no good way back.
Out the window, on the ledge
doves murmur. The moon is the color of ash.
The wind is coming this way again.
I see it playing among the shining limbs
of the olives, shy behind the window glass
and the sheer, crinoline curtain.
And that perfect dark—it's ruining color.
It's waiting right over there
beyond the trees, clinging to the breeze
with long, terrible fingers.
But, you'd better stay here—
where else can you look for love?

On a Balcony with the *Lunch Poems*

The sun kneels on the landscape.
      The sky is chalked.
Helicopters—

nevertheless, it's lunch time
      so I'm here for some fish,
some good bread and olives.

In the distance: the gold-domed palace,
      black prayer flags,
bright rows of laundry, hanging.

They're smiling
      as they bring it all up.
There is wine.

A boy playing hooky
      (is the school on fire *again*?)
splashes in a fountain

and everyone laughs,
      because god
would've wanted us to.

They say someone's dying—
      right now and brutally,
deep in the village.
      They carry up more wine.

Down in the courtyard
      the Bangladeshi
fertilizes something
      with his good hand,
clears away last night's *mut'ah* marriage contracts.

This in the news today:

       ... a fatwa to burn every church,
destroy all Buddhas and saints.

       and

       Strictly no sale or usage
of tampons at the airport.

Meanwhile ... a woman lifts
       her *niqab* and sips. Smoldering
tires. Someone's unloading yams.

I get up to find the toilet.
       The *azan* pierces the afternoon,
a lost nuthatch panics on the railing.

An apron of tear gas
       (made in America) snowing,
a man face-down, praying.
       In southern California, my sons enduring
the accident that is their mother.

I remember loving
       the way their faces
looked when I pushed
       the red plastic swing
roped to the high limb
       of the willow. Oh, the creaking
creaking,

       always the going,
always the returning,
       the four of them wearing
Superman underwear.

Previous Winners of the John Ciardi Prize for Poetry

One Blackbird at a Time By Wendy Barker, selected by Alice Friman
Border States by Jane Hoogestraat, selected by Luis J. Rodriguez
Beauty Mark by Suzanne Cleary, selected by Kevin Prufer
Axis Mundi by Karen Holmberg, selected by Lorna Dee Cervantes
Secret Wounds by Richard M. Berlin, selected by Gary Young
Mapmaking by Megan Harlan, selected by Sidney Wade
Tongue of War: From Pearl Harbor to Nagasaki by Tony Barnstone,
    selected by B. H. Fairchild
Black Tupelo Country by Doug Ramspeck,
    selected by Leslie Adrienne Miller
Airs & Voices by Paula Bonnell, selected by Mark Jarman
Wayne's College of Beauty by David Swanger,
    selected by Colleen J. McElroy
The Portable Famine by Rane Arroyo, selected by Robin Becker
Fence Line by Curtis Bauer, selected by Christopher Buckley
Escape Artist by Terry Blackhawk, selected by Molly Peacock
Kentucky Swami by Tim Skeen, selected by Michael Burns
The Resurrection Machine by Steve Gehrke, selected by Miller Williams

Bonnie Bolling's first collection of poetry, *In the Kingdom of the Sons*, won the Liam Rector First Book Prize for Poetry, and her second, *The Red Hijab*, won the John Ciardi Poetry Prize. She was awarded fellowships by Bread Loaf Writers Conferences, Prague Summer Writers and the University of California, Riverside, where she received a MFA. Her play, *The Red Hijab*, was produced at UCR by Playworks in 2010. Bonnie is editor-in-chief of *Verdad* and lives in southern California and the Persian Gulf.